Stepping Over the Threshold

I0190786

By Bob Mumford

LIFECHANGERS®

P.O. Box 3709 ❖ Cookeville, TN 3ξ
931.520.3730 ❖ lc@lifechangers.(

P.
(8
Al
IS
© .
All
Prir

Stepping Over the Threshold

By Bob Mumford

Probably the most dramatic transition in my natural life occurred on my 20th birthday, December 29, 1950, as I stepped across the threshold into the Navy recruiting center in Atlantic City, New Jersey. Upon being sworn in two things became painfully obvious. First, my life was no longer my own! For the foreseeable future every aspect of personal life would be subservient to the needs of the Navy. My "personal sovereignty" had vanished like a puff of smoke.

Second, my whole world was about to change radically. I was thrust into a totally foreign environment for which I was absolutely unprepared. An unhappy looking chief petty officer yelled at our group of new recruits, "Get down there and clamp your toes on the bottom rung of the ladder!" Befuddled, none of us had a clue this was Navy-talk for "stand on the last step of the stairs."

Over the course of the next six weeks at the Great Lakes Naval Training Center, I was transformed from civilian to seaman. The changes I was required to embrace were more dramatic and more costly than words can convey. Radical seems too weak to describe the idea of no longer belonging to yourself. Once I was able to make the transition,

I loved the Navy. Apart from my dramatic call to ministry, I would probably have made it my career. It all began when I made the decision to step over a threshold.

Hear me, if you possibly can, I am deeply convinced that the Body of Christ, the nation, and our global culture may be standing at a threshold that demarcates a transition into a radically different spiritual, social, and cultural environment.

Transition is different from change. Change is not an option, it is a constant! In the Navy my function and behavior often changed to fit circumstances. As a pharmacist mate on the USS *Aludra,* a five hold refrigeration ship, I patched up minor wounds, dispensed medications, and patiently listened as shipmates griped about the Navy. I was responsible for much of the administration of our sickbay with endless paperwork and constant logistics. At mess, local bars, or playing poker, I was just one of the guys. When I came back to the Lord after 12 years of backsliding, I became an unofficial chaplain of our ship. Each "function" required that I change my behavior and thinking; however, whatever I was doing I was a US Navy sailor through and through.

Since the Reformation, churches have gone through many changes, but their essential form and nature have stayed the same. I believe we now stand at a *threshold,* a transition. I refer to this as a *Kairos moment,* a term which I will explain more fully moving forward.

In this *Plumbline* I will help identify the historical significance of this current threshold. May we find freedom to embrace this transition into the spiritual and the cultural environments now occurring. My convictions about the nature of this transition are presented with the hope that they may enable us to discover supernatural ability in Christ. We are learning to rest in His purpose without yielding to fear: not becoming focused on forecasts of gloom or glory; not being caught up in conspiracy theories chasing rumors and half-truths. All of these only lead to false centers.

Thresholds

A threshold may be defined as "the magnitude or intensity that must be exceeded for a certain reaction, phenomenon, result, or condition to occur or be manifested."[1] An example would be a pot of water heating on a stove. As the temperature rises we may notice few changes, but when the water reaches 212° F it will begin to boil. The boiling threshold has been reached.

Our threshold may occur as a result of many changes, some seen and some unseen. It may occur over years or even decades. At some point, however, we will have crossed a threshold. We may only recognize it once we have embraced and crossed into that which is yet to come.

Forces, both good and evil, have been loosed.

---

1 Oxford Dictionary

We are going to be faced with changes that cannot be avoided. They will demand critical decisions and spiritual maturity. The challenge can be described as: *what will need to change?* If the changes are dramatic and comprehensive, how will we know the difference between needed changes and biblical compromise? We will be required to respond, evaluate, and engage concepts that we have never engaged before.

How do we prepare? How must we adapt as we stand at this threshold? What will happen if we don't? John the Baptist was a case in point. He was not part of the Old Covenant, but strangely, he was unable to become part of the Kingdom that was unfolding. He, in a manner similar to our own, was spanning two very different eras. One was being dismantled. The other was not yet fully revealed or functioning. John had declared of Jesus:

> He will baptize you with the Holy Spirit and fire. His winnowing fork is in His hand, and He will thoroughly clear His threshing floor; and He will gather His wheat into the barn, but He will burn up the chaff with unquenchable fire.[2]

Later when John did not recognize the fiery Messiah he expected, he sent his disciples to Jesus to ask, "Are you the expected one or shall we look

2 Matthew 3:11-12

for someone else?" Jesus had replied, "Blessed is he who keeps from stumbling over me.[3]" John stood at a threshold, but could not step over. His Old Covenant presuppositions could not handle the form in which the New Covenant was appearing. Jesus declared in the synagogue:

> The spirit of the lord is upon me,
> Because he anointed me to preach the gospel to the poor.
> He has sent me to proclaim release to the captives,
> And recovery of sight to the blind,
> To set free those who are oppressed,
> To proclaim the favorable year of the lord.[4]

Jesus was preparing those who could hear Him for drastic change, the type and magnitude none of them were expecting. Being birthed into a new perspective is not easy and is often painful, but it is essential if we are to grow and embrace the future with strength and clarity. The pain and pressure of transition causes us to re-examine our foundational belief systems. We must be ever willing to "trade our pearls[5]". We let go of that which is passing away while we embrace the new threshold. When it does not fit into our presuppositional, theological,

---

3 Matthew 11:1-6
4 Luke 4:18-19
5 Matthew 13:46

or religious boxes, we risk stumbling or being scandalized.

Living in South Florida for many years allowed our family to become all too familiar with hurricanes. The reality was not *if* you would experience a hurricane, but *when* you would experience a hurricane. Often with a storm barreling up the Caribbean we would prepare with storm shutters. We gathered everything we would need to weather the effects of the storm winds and possibly live for an extended period without electricity and running water. Because we lived close to the ocean we could be forced to evacuate if a storm of certain intensity was expected. Those who prepared did well. Those who did not prepare sometimes paid with their lives, as is often witnessed when major storms ravaged the Florida and Gulf Coast areas.

This *Plumbline* is written from within the storm of the Covid-19 pandemic. Multiple epidemiologists warned that it was not a matter of *if* the storm would come, but *when* it would come. Much of the world was unprepared, and it is difficult to discern the economic and social impact that may ultimately be more traumatic than the actual pandemic. Regardless of where we find ourselves five or ten years from now, that which I wish to share will be applicable. As we embrace the changes confronting us, we must step over the threshold regardless of what other storms may present themselves.

Personally, I have been in a decade long period

of "birth pangs". Being prophetic in my calling and temperament I not only see what God is doing, I often experience it in my person. The Spirit labors with *"groanings too deep for words.[6]"* I believe my own experience of travail has been associated with these processes and/or transitions:

1) My own growth as a maturing son.
2) The increasing realization that the institutions we lean on to "keep us safe," may ultimately become our prisons.
3) The "birth pangs of creation" longing to be freed from the inexorable process of corruption.
4) The tumultuous, complex transition of the Kingdom being extracted from its present religious context.

I am aware that I am not standing alone at this threshold. Others are also experiencing a disquieting sense of an impending transition into an era that we cannot accurately foresee or fully understand. I have come to value "relational safety" as a source of balance, adjustment, and encouragement. That which I understand, as at least a portion of the mind of the Lord, has been confirmed in the parallel journeys of other men and women. Therefore, I feel

6 Romans 8:26

that many of you reading this will find a resonate chord with our shared experience.

1. Maturing sons and daughters

When I was a newly converted and un-churched sailor, I was immediately impacted by the message of the Kingdom of God (used 151 times in the New Testament, 14 of which are in Paul's epistles). I read it as the dominate theme of Christ's message. Oh how I longed to understand and embrace what seemed to be hidden in this mystery. Jesus called it the "pearl" and the "treasure" that was worth paying any price to fully inherit. My prayer (which you are free to borrow) became, *Lord Jesus, please do not leave me to myself.*

Maturity requires that we radically shift our motivation and focus. We move from bless me and do for me to Father how may I please you and fulfill your intended desires for my life? The healing and Charismatic outpourings of the last century immeasurably advanced the redemptive process of history, but unfortunately it has opened the door to a self-referential, entitlement mentality. I believe this is part of the correctional threshold we are now experiencing. Jesus is leading us into an era in which His bride possesses the inheritance prepared for her since the foundation of the world. The process can be painful and pressing at times, but Paul reminds us that by "many tribulations we must enter the kingdom of God.[7]" The forming of human spirit—in labor until Christ is formed in you.[8] The spirit of the Son cries "Abba". Only in the garden did Jesus use these words. It is a relational cry to know the Father!

Through the Old Testament, I have become aware of a thread that gives me courage to press forward. The Hebrew word, *chaciyd* or *hesed* (used 32 times in the OT, Strong's #2623) is usually translated holy one, saint, or godly one in English translations. Its meaning is different from the Hebrew word *qodesh* (used 464 times in the OT, Strong's #6944) and always translated holy.

The intent of *chaciyd* is "kindness or favor, or free grace—never that of mercy in the sense of compassion."[9] *Chaciyd* "should denote a kindly loved one, a dearly loved one, a favored one, one who is in favor, a favorite one, who is the object of gracious love and is treated accordingly. That is, it denotes a person in whom loving-kindness is thought of as resident."[10]

It gives us strong security and courage to know that we are not only recipients of God's grace, which

7 Acts 14:22

8 Galatians 4:19

9 *The Prophets and the Promise,* p. 313. Rev. Willis Judson Beecher, D.D.; Professor of Hebrew language and literature, Theological Seminary of Auburn in the State of New York. Copyright 1905 by Beecher. Thomas W. Crowell & Co. publishers.

10 Ibid, p. 314.

He offers to all humanity, but *individually* looked upon with loving-kindness and favor because the Father has foreknown me (Bob Mumford) and *insert YOUR name* from the foundation of the world! He has predestined us to be conformed to the image of His Son. He has called us, chosen us, justified us, and caused us to sit at His right hand as favored sons and daughters![11] As I personalize *chaciyd* I am empowered with a sense of HIS power working in me to lay hold of His purpose for me at the threshold of the coming manifestation of His glory.

2) Institutions of this world may become prisons

Most of my life I went merrily about my business without any immediate means of communication with my family, office, or fellow workers. If something urgent needed to be communicated I would have to hunt for a pay phone. Long distance communication, for the most part, was transacted by mail necessitating days of waiting.

Today, if I am away from home without my cell phone, a certain level of angst rises in the back of my mind, "What if . . . ?" When the internet goes out it is like a door slams shut on vital communications. I feel "unplugged" and stifled. These once novel gadgets that I have come to depend upon, in a sense, have taken me prisoner. I can scarcely function without them. We can become prisoners of our own creations.

11 See Romans 8:29-30

Our institutions have been created to provide for our needs and to protect us from the perils of life. Consider how intimately these institutions have affected our lives: health care; law enforcement; schools and universities; public utilities; the armed forces; communications and news industries; banking; finance; civil government; and religious institutions. None of these institutions are essentially malevolent or malicious in their primary purpose, but they may become substitutes for a rock-solid foundation in the Kingdom of God. They may hamper the Kingdom's ability to supply our needs and sense of security.

During the Covid-19 pandemic, we have witnessed how interdependent, fragile, and vulnerable these institutions are. The above mentioned institutions were affected to one degree or another. We do not know how our "safety structures" will fare in the next few years. Ultimately they are all shifting sand.

Religious and spiritual institutions may likewise be deeply shaken. We may be confronted with aspects of Christ's Kingdom that are not included as the scriptural norm of our church, theological persuasion, or Biblical interpretation. Presuppositions we hold as inviolate may be challenged.

Jesus' security was the unshakable rock of His relationship with His Father. He found no security from His friends, His followers, the religious institutions, or the civil government. His security and hope was drawn from His single purpose—*to please His Father.* Everything else was secondary. The centrality of His purpose gave Him the ability to freely and perfectly embrace His Father first. He remained unentangled by created institutions and false centers.

"Purpose" occurs 38 times in the New American Standard translation representing different Greek words and phrases. The moment we lose purpose we lose hope. When we lose purpose and hope we are in spiritual trouble. We cannot have hope without purpose. Jesus refused all false centers. He had surrendered His personal sovereignty to the Father.

Now, God the Father has given us the spirit of His Son.[12] The spirit is centered on the same purpose as Jesus, to please the Father, crying "Abba! Father!" Christ's presence *in us* then seeks to fill us with the hope of glory.[13] Christ's purpose kept him Father-centered. He never lost, compromised, or played games with it. Maintaining that center cost Him everything. Most personal spiritual warfare is the effort to move us off of this center. In His passion in the garden Jesus yielded His personal sovereignty to the Father, "Not as I wish, but as You wish."[14] His spirit within us continually urges us toward the same center.

---

12 See Romans 8:15 and Galatians 4:6
13 Colossians 1:27.
14 Matthew 26:39, Greek

I know men and women who have been given legitimate visions about what God wants them to do. They have lived by that vision and done well because they have insisted upon pleasing the Father at the center of that vision. They did not allow the vision to become the center in and of itself. If I have 10,000 people in a church building and that becomes my center, I will lose my purpose to please the Father. It signifies that I am headed for trouble.

God is glorified by people whose purpose is pleasing Father.

3) Birth pangs of creation longing to be freed from corruption

As children of God, we are destined in some mysterious manner to participate in the reversal of creation's corruption. Creation includes all things, both spiritual and natural. Paul tells us "the *whole* creation groans and suffers the pains of childbirth." Paul seems to infer in Romans 8 that we also share in its groaning.[15]

I believe there is a deeper spiritual connection with creation than the Western mindset of "scientific materialism" has been willing to acknowledge. Quantum physics has begun to demonstrate that there is interconnectedness in the structure of the Universe that is in some sense, spiritual. The great mystics throughout history have understood this. To varying degrees we feel the pain of all creation and

15 See Romans 8:18-23

participate in it without always being aware of it.

Because we have seen ourselves as essentially separate from creation we have felt free to place more emphasis on subduing creation than we have on cultivating and keeping it. Mankind's unbridled greed and hubris have projected its spiritual corruption into the natural creation to a disastrous level. Dying oceans; deforestation; species extinctions; and the poisoning of land, water, and air bear witness to our inability to steward the gift God has given us. I find increasing grief and internal groaning as I watch our beautiful world suffer in the name of "progress".

When Christ was resurrected through the power of the Father He began "making all things new."[16] He does not say He is making all new things. In Jesus' resurrection He was not given a new body. His existing body (as identified by the wounds of the cross) was made new. His resurrection released a transforming power into creation that reverses the force of corruption and entropy. It restores and renews all that it touches. Wherever the Kingdom comes, it affects transformation.

Through maturing as sons and daughters, we experience the birthing of the fullness of Christ's resurrection in our own persons as a new creation. Likewise, we are each participating in the groaning of this present creation as it awaits the revelation of the glory of the Bride of Christ.

---

16 Revelation 21:5

4) **Extraction of the Kingdom from its present religious context**

Let me make it clear: *I am not anti-church.* I am centered on Christ and His Kingdom. In general this is a centrality that has been forgotten, dismissed, or refused. This is witnessed by the strange fact that none of the great creeds of the Church mention the Kingdom of God as a major theme of the gospel. Jesus' admonition was to put His Kingdom first and let everything else be added!

I am deeply convicted that this present threshold is the transition out of a 500-year season in Church history. Much of what has been embraced as "the Scriptural norm" within the Church is being challenged and modified. In 1994 I locked myself up with sixteen books on Church History with the determination to understand the pattern of its progress from Pentecost to our present day. I discovered that since its birth the Church has gone through a major and often convulsive transition approximately every 500 years. Somewhat surprisingly, I discovered that much of society was often sharing in the same spasms of transition.

These periods of transition may be many decades or even centuries in length, and they are usually marked by a single or series of specific events. These events are surrounded by what I came to understand as *Kairos*[17] *moments.* A Kairos moment

---

17 *Kairos* is a New Testament Greek word translated "season" but most often "time." It means a time of defined

is a mega transition in history that transforms an entire culture—political, economic, social, and religious—from one foundation to another. It is typified by chaos in varying degrees; challenging of the status quo; changing and restructuring; making all things new.

My dear wife Judith will periodically sort out her clothes closet. That which is out of style or worn out will be discarded or given to the local thrift store. That which is still useful she will return to the closet for continued use. It may also occasion a shopping trip to replace the discarded garments. Jesus spoke to this process when He said, "Every scribe [member of the established system] who has become a disciple of the kingdom of heaven [embraced the transition] is like a head of a household, who brings out of his treasure things new and old [part of the old but useful in the new]."[18] Those who understand the Kairos moment and are able to embrace the required changes will prosper; those who cannot will atrophy.

There have been four mega-transitions in the history of the Church, each roughly 500 years in duration, which are presented by the following illustrations. I will not pretend to give an extensive presentation of Church history, but it is important to understand our present place in the purposes of God.

---

length as opposed to *chronos* which implies time in a more general sense.
18 Matthew 13:52

We use an arch to represent each 500 year period. An era rises to an apex of influence and then begins to lose its vitality as the age progresses and/or it becomes subject to the forces of corruption. In the dynamics of the transition the seeds of the coming era are sown and begin to sprout before the former age leaves the scene. We have a demonstration of this dynamic in the Old Testament as the kingdom was passed from Saul to David. God was preparing David to become the next king before He rejected Saul. As Saul lost his ability to reign, David was in place to ascend to the throne.

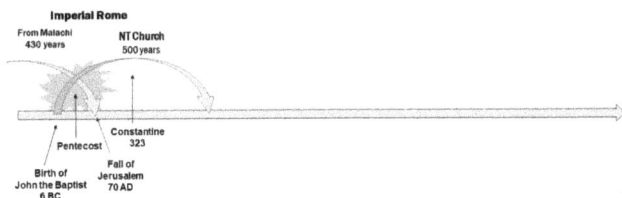

Church Age in 500 Year Increments

The *Kairos Moment* is a mega-transition in history

Imperial Rome

From Malachi 430 years

NT Church 500 years

Constantine 323

Pentecost

Fall of Jerusalem 70 AD

Birth of John the Baptist 6 BC

The first illustration represents roughly the first 500 years of the Church. It shows the transition from the Jewish era as the focus of God's purposes to that of the Church. The intersection of the two is surrounded by a Kairos moment indicated by the star burst. When John the Baptist stepped into history it marked the beginning of a transition into a new age. It culminated in the fall of Jerusalem and the end of temple expression of Judaism with the animal sacrificial system. The New Testament and the historian Josephus gave witness to this transition in graphic and painful detail.

It is worthy to note that during this general period of history the classical culture became more Hellenized with the conquests of Alexander the Great. Rome doubled the size of its empire to include most of Europe and North Africa. Wherever Rome conquered, it imported both the Roman and adopted Greek cultures. It was a period of enormous change, which laid the foundations of Western culture.

The followers of the new Christian faith traveled through the Roman world, and the church influenced most of the known world before the fall of Jerusalem. The early church was organic, energized by the Holy Spirit, and oriented toward the Kingdom of God. Through a natural course of growth the church developed a leadership structure, but it was a living organism and thrived in spite of horrific persecutions.

In 313 AD the newly converted Roman Emperor Constantine issued the Edict of Milan ending the persecution of the church. In 323 he made Christianity the official religion of the Empire. Even though the church may have breathed a collective sigh of relief to be freed from persecution, it soon found itself being molded by the Roman culture. The church was "Latinized" in language, and it became an imperial church.

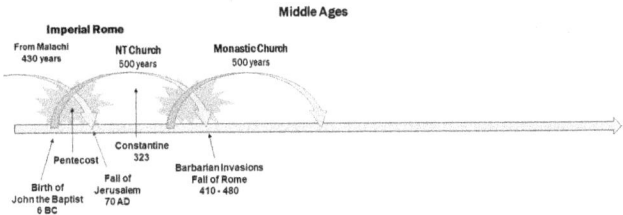

Church Age in 500 Year Increments

The *Kairos Moment* is a mega-transition in history

Middle Ages

Imperial Rome

From Malachi
430 years

NT Church
500 years

Monastic Church
500 years

Pentecost

Constantine
323

Birth of
John the Baptist
6 BC

Fall of
Jerusalem
70 AD

Barbarian Invasions
Fall of Rome
410 - 480

The barbarian tribes of Europe began to invade the Roman Empire in the late 300's. In 410 Rome was sacked by Visigoths. The loss of Roman culture and the encroachment of paganism inaugurated a period characterized by cultural stagnation and superstition, later to be labeled misleadingly as the Dark Ages. At this Kairos juncture, the church retained its formal structure. Most of its vitality was preserved in monasteries and convents. In the ensuing centuries these became centers of learning, social and economic stability, and cultural preservation.

Prior to Constantine, the Roman Empire had been divided into Eastern and Western halves for more efficient government. Over the centuries the church developed along similar lines. The Western church became more Latinized through the influence of Roman culture. The Eastern (Orthodox or Greek) church continued to formalize, though the world view would retain more similarities to its early roots.

The Roman Church was ruled by the Pope from Rome and the Orthodox church by the Patriarch from Constantinople. The tension between the two branches of Christianity came to a head in 1054 when the Roman pope and the Orthodox patriarch mutually excommunicated each other. The intricacies of the differences between the two are unnecessary for us to understand. However, it must be noted that the influence of the Pope in Europe continued to expand until over the course of the next 500 years. The power of the Papacy and the Roman church in western and central Europe was almost total. The influence of the Orthodox church had been somewhat reduced because of the Islamic conquest of Asia Minor culminating with the fall of Constantinople to the Ottoman Turks in 1465.

Our historical focus will now be limited to the history of the Western, Latinized Roman church. It was the foundation of European culture that carried forward into Protestantism and spread around the world in the age of Colonialism.

Church Age in 500 Year Increments

The *Kairos Moment* is a mega-transition in history

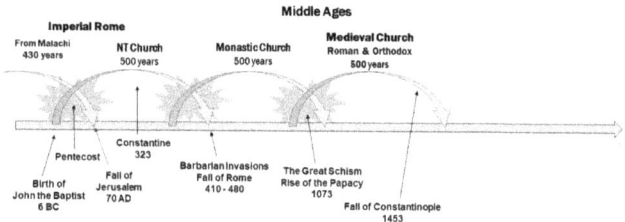

Middle Ages

Imperial Rome			**Medieval Church**
From Malachi 430 years	NT Church 500 years	Monastic Church 500 years	Roman & Orthodox 500 years

Constantine 323

Pentecost

Birth of John the Baptist 6 BC

Fall of Jerusalem 70 AD

Barbarian Invasions Fall of Rome 410 - 480

The Great Schism Rise of the Papacy 1073

Fall of Constantinople 1453

Tragically, the observation that *power tends to corrupt* held true for the Roman church over the course of the next five centuries. The pressures for change (in practice, doctrine, and power) in the Roman Church had been building for decades. The lid was taken off the cooker, so to speak, by Martin Luther in 1517. The resulting explosion changed the course of history forever. Chaos ensued resulted in a series of religious wars that shook the secular powers and left millions dead in their wake.

The surrounding Kairos moment included monumental change, along with unrest in every area of life. Copernicus and Galileo discovered the earth was not the center of the solar system. They were condemned by the church resulting in an ever-widening intellectual divorce of science and faith. The discoveries of the New World energized the Western nations into a race of conquest, colonialism, and imperialism. This period also gave birth to the Renaissance and to the Enlightenment. This further marginalized the influence of a biblical world view and laid the foundations of the modern age.

The church has gone through many changes in the last 500 years, rearranging furniture in the house but is now crossing a threshold into an uncharted environment. The people of God must embrace some radical changes if we are to see the Kingdom emerge and impact a hurting world in the purposes of God.

Church Age in 500 Year Increments

The *Kairos Moment* is a mega-transition in history

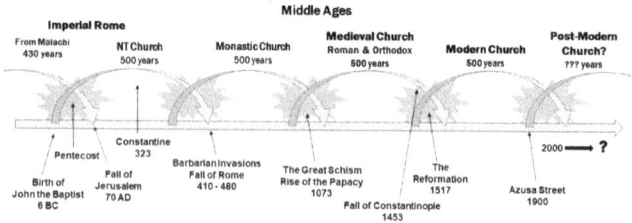

I am not alone in these observations. In *The Great Emergence,* author and editor Phyllis Tickle notes that every 500 years or so the Church is compelled to hold a "rummage sale". Many existing structures and traditions "must be shattered in order that renewal and new growth may occur."[19] She also observes that we "see over and over again, religious enthusiasms in all holy rummage sales are unfailingly symptomatic or expressive of concomitant political, economic, and social upheavals."[20]

Having lived many years in Florida I became happily acquainted with the Florida Lobster (aka Spiny or Rock Lobster), which being a seafood lover, I enjoyed whenever possible. The Florida Lobster, like its northern cousin, lives in a shell, technically an exoskeleton that gives it protection and mobility. However, as the lobster grows it must periodically molt and shed its shell in order to continue growing.

19 Tickle, Phyllis. *The Great Emergence*. Baker
Publishing Group. Kindle Edition. Loc. 154.
20 Ibid. Loc. 197

The new, living lobster must leave the dead shell behind and move on.

The Church for 2000 years has been like a lobster. As it grows and changes it must molt. Its shell can no longer contain it. During this Kairos moment of molting there is a choice to be made—stay with the dead shell (which is familiar and safe) or move forward with the new life that may be vulnerable. The Jewish followers of Jesus faced this moment in the first century, the followers of the Reformation faced it, and I believe we are facing it in this present generation.

Since World War II, history has transitioned from the modern world view to a foundation that has yet to be named but is simply called "post-modern." Below are four characteristics of the modern world view that are especially relevant to the Church as it has moved forward over the last five hundred years:

- Absolutism of truth
- Institutions as the foundation of social organization and identification: corporate, religious, societial, etc.
- Secular science and materialism as the foundation of knowledge and "truth"
- Rationalism and knowledge as a basis of action
- Mechanistic, Newtonian world view

In contrast, the post-modern world view has

begun to morph into one that may be described as:

- Relativistic: truth and reality may be different depending on the circumstances and world view
- Non-institutional: networks, relationships, philosophies, and common belief systems are the basis of social identity and organization
- Existential: openness to spiritual, mystical; experience, intuition, and synergetic thinking are more of a basis of world view and action
- "Quantum" world view: non-mechanistic, non-empirical, spiritual foundation to the Universe

As we compare these two lists, we can see why the Christian message embedded in a modern world view has become increasingly difficult for a post-modern culture to embrace. It simply runs contrary to much of what our contemporary culture holds to be real and true. I am exceedingly hopeful as I see new expressions of the Body of Christ taking shape around the world. I have the utmost confidence that the Holy Spirit is causing a fresh manifestation of the Body of Christ to emerge. A manifestation that will be a more perfect expression of the Kingdom of God.

That being said, I believe there is embryonic

evidence that we may be coming to the close of a 2000-year epoch. The all-inclusive nature of God's redemptive purposes may be transformed into something so different, it may become almost unrecognizable. We are possibly being extracted from all that "Christianity" currently is as an institutional religion. Will we embrace a manifestation of the Kingdom of God that is more organic and relational? Will we embrace a Kingdom that more adequately expresses Father's purposes in the earth?

Whatever form emerges, it may not be within our ability to understand what God has up His sleeve for the coming era. As Jesus stood at the threshold of a new era with His disciples, He told them, "I have many more things to say to you, but you cannot bear them now."[21] If Jesus had given them a preview of what was to come in the course of the next 40 years they would have been scandalized. They were so fixed in what they understood as the eternality of the Jewish system that they could not have conceived that they were approaching the end of their own age.

God's redemptive purposes had been centered in the Jewish people and the nation of Israel for close to 2000 years.[22] The Jewish people would continue, but the temple worship with it sacrificial system

---

21 John 16:12
22 I base this on the call of Abraham which was in roughly 2000 BC.

given by the Mosaic covenant a millennia and a half previously would come to an end in 70 AD. Could it be that the threshold we are about to cross is so transformational that we would stumble at the sight of what is on the other side? If the disciples could not have envisioned what was to come, then why should we think we can? Could it be that God is about to reveal a dimension of the Kingdom that would alter our understanding of His redemptive plan? I *am not* saying it *will* happen; I just wonder if . . .

Where Are We?

Since the first century, believers have been looking for the bodily return of Christ. In every era of Church history there have been sincere, godly men and women who looked at the present events and concluded that the "signs of the times" indicated the return of Jesus was near. A continued effort finds context in the "prophetic scriptures" to give bearing as to where we are in relation to the end of the age. When I taught the book of Revelation in Bible College, I had the entire sequence of events neatly outlined on nine blackboards that circled the room. I was in heaven! Later I was compelled to re-examine my handiwork. I was forced to acknowledge that most of it no longer made sense.

There have been schemas of end time scenarios with myriads of scriptural charts, predictions, and time lines that had to be redrawn and modified when

Jesus failed to appear. Longing for the coming[23] of the Lord is a legitimate, biblical motivation. However, some suffer under an obsessive fixation on current signs of the times. This often produces short-timer mentalities; escapism; or morbid fixations on evil or disaster and the temporal "judgments of God." These *false centers* can lead to a withdrawal from the world and a lack of personal responsibility for the practical application of the Kingdom for a hurting world.

Bible scholars of Jesus' day read the prophetic scriptures so selectively that they totally missed the advent of their long-awaited Messiah, even becoming His persecutors. Because of their "biblical" presuppositions they were blind to Jesus as the Messiah. He was mysteriously hidden in the Law and the Prophets. They built bible boxes that became inescapable mental prisons.

Jesus is coming again! But perhaps He is coming within a set of circumstances or in a manner that we have not considered. How we see the future affects how we conduct ourselves in the present. We must be exceedingly circumspect that our biblical boxes do not become our mental prisons.

I have chosen not allow myself to entertain suppositions about what the other side of this threshold may look like. I do not want to create expectations in my own mind to shape my interpretation of Scripture and my understanding of

23 Greek *Parousia.* Can also be translated "presence."

the full intention of God's redemptive plan. I am encouraged by the emergence of a generation of Christians who have the Kingdom priority as their life focus. They are willing to spend themselves to see the spiritual Kingdom emerge in the nations apart from religious and institutional constraints.

After nearly 70 years of proclamation, my own eschatology is centered in God's *people* rather than in world events. *Circumstances do not and will not precipitate His coming.* The Spirit and the Bride, in oneness, will be saying: "Come, Lord Jesus." This is not a cry for us to be caught away from some form of tribulation. It is the desire for the consummation of *Agape* when the Bride has made herself ready.

The Shaking of all Things

God will shake all created things that can be shaken for the revealing of His uncreated, unshakable Kingdom to emerge.

And His voice shook the earth then, [On Mt. Sinai] but now He has promised, saying, "*Yet once more I will shake not only the earth, but also the heaven.*" This expression, "Yet once more," denotes the removing of those things which can be shaken, as of created things, so that those things which cannot be shaken may remain. Therefore, since we receive a kingdom which cannot be shaken, let us show gratitude, by which we may offer to God an acceptable service with reverence and awe; for our God is a consuming fire.[24]

Hear this passage vividly presented from *The Message* translation:

His voice that time shook the earth to its foundations; this time—he's told us this quite plainly—he'll also rock the heavens: "One last shaking, from top to bottom, stem to stern." The phrase "one last shaking" means a thorough housecleaning, getting rid of all the historical and religious junk so that the unshakable essentials stand clear and uncluttered.

Do you see what we've got? An unshakable kingdom! And do you see how thankful we must be? Not only thankful, but brimming with worship, deeply reverent before God. For God is not an indifferent bystander. He is actively cleaning house, torching all that needs to burn, and he won't quit until it's all cleansed. God himself is Fire!

What will remain after all else is shaken lose? Shaking is not and will not be fun. We are watching our entire world system being shaken by a virus,

24 Hebrews 12:26-29, italics mine

and as of this writing we do not yet know how much of the present structure will collapse or remain.

Picture a beautiful modern city devastated by an 8.5 magnitude earthquake. Some buildings would be reduced to rubble, some would need to be demolished, and some would need extensive repair. *Except one*--one building, which may not have appeared different from all the rest, would be revealed as having something within its internal structure that allowed it to stand when all other structures collapsed.

So it will be with the shaking of "all things." Many institutions and entities may collapse, some may simply no longer function, and others may need to be reconfigured to function in a new environment. The one governmental entity that has not and cannot collapse is the eternal Kingdom of our Lord Jesus. "Of the increase of His government, there shall be no end.[25]" The uncreated Kingdom will endure forever.

The question for us is whether the "reality" on which we rest our lives consists of realities we have created (social, economic, intellectual, theological, or even Biblical) or in the uncreated reality of His Kingdom?

Uncreated reality is the identity and essence of the Kingdom. Kingdom reality reigns in and through: *Agape* (which is the prime mover of all things in God); *light* (which brings order to cha-

---

25 Isaiah 9:7

os and truth to confusion); and *spirit* (which gives life)[26]. The essence of the Kingdom transforms all *created reality*.

Within Christian thought there are realities that have been "created" to express a particular understanding of our experience with God. Some are closer to the uncreated reality than others. These realities may prove to be adequate for a season, but seasons change. Systems do not become wrong, merely inadequate to meet the present situations. This is a concept I would ask you to grasp and retain for navigating the present transitions we are facing.

Within "shaking" something new may come forth. God revealed uncreated reality in the person of His Son. We tend to create a conceptual "shell" around our understanding of His Kingdom. Eventually we become more committed to the shell than to the Person. When this happens, God in His mercy initiates a rummage sale. It is time for the lobster to molt the shell and continue to grow.

God has children whom we may be unable or unwilling to recognize, let alone receive. As the Father of all humanity,[27] God may bring others

---

26 There are three "God is" statements which express the very essence of His being and nature. "God is spirit (John 4:25)"; "God is light (1 John 1:5); and "God is love (1 John 4:7).

27 *"The Father, from whom every family* [Gk. "fatherhood"] *in heaven and on earth derives its name"* (Ephesians 3:14-15). *"The living God, who is the Savior of all men, especially of believers"* (1 Timothy 4:10).

by a different path than the one you have been travelling. Judith and I have four children. It is totally impossible to relate to each the same due to differences in personality and response. God must be seen functioning as a Father. He is *relational.* He responds to each as need and circumstances demand. We are to demonstrate *faith that works by love, not primarily by doctrinal formula.*

The Wheat and the Tares

The wheat and the tares will grow together until the harvest,[28] which is the consummation of the age. We are watching the tares of fallen human behavior mature as increasing corruption worldwide, but I do not think we can approach the end of the age until the wheat has come to some form of maturity. We are to be conformed to the image of the Son and fill the earth with the knowledge of the glory of the Lord. At this point, at least in the West, the wheat and tares can be hard to tell apart.

Maturity of His Body

The children of God will grow up into mature sons and daughters for the purpose of setting Creation free from slavery to corruption and death in all its forms.[29]

The status of the present-day Church is not wrong or evil, it is simply inadequate for what the Lord intends to do in the next phase of reconciling

28 Matthew 13:36-43.
29 Rom. 8:19-21

all things to Himself. To become adequate it will be essential to cease using God as a utilitarian tool to meet our needs and weaponizing Scripture. We must continue to sell all and buy the whole field. As we freely embrace Christ, who seeks to take us into an uncreated, *relational* reality, the *rhema* of the Holy Spirit will penetrate deeply into our innermost beings. He will accomplish His intended and necessary transformation in us.

We must grasp spiritual discipline as the purifying work of the Holy Spirit and God's *merciful* judgements. His judgements are never punitive; they are purifying. If we truly understand this, we will welcome them! To allow Him to shift our thinking may require releasing our inadequate personal and religious presuppositions.

Jesus told us to make disciples. I have known multitudes of "saved" people (some of whom I pastored) who by their attitudes and actions would be most difficult to identify as disciples of Jesus.

There is ample biblical evidence in the Scripture that He must come *in* His saints before He will come *for* His saints. An invisible Kingdom can only become visible when those claiming to know Him demonstrate His prevailing presence. It is Father's intent that His people become an incarnation of His nature in the same manner as Jesus. The nature of the Kingdom as 'Signs of the Kingdom' has been designed to make the invisible Kingdom seen and embraced.

For many of you who are experiencing some measure of these same birth pangs, let me encourage you that the future will be victorious! However, it is not necessarily triumphalistic. Paul makes this clear in he writes to the Romans,

> Who will separate us from the love of Christ? Will tribulation, or distress, or persecution, or famine, or nakedness, or peril, or sword? But *in* all these things we overwhelmingly conquer through Him who loved us. [30] [Italics mine]

Paul states that we conquer in the things (victorious), but not necessarily over these things (triumphant). This is not to say we will never be triumphant, but to insist we will always come out on top of every difficult circumstance is neither biblical nor realistic.

Quantum Spirituality

The reality of the spiritual universe is often pictured in the natural. In recent years I have become familiar (quite inadequately) with quantum physics. Isaac Newton formulated and tested mathematically the laws of a three dimensional universe. He was empirical in his approach working from materialistic presuppositions. Einstein introduced us to a deeper understanding of the Universe with his theories of

30 Rom 8:35 & 37

special and general relativity. The laws and equations of Newton and Einstein described the nature of the observable universe. However, these same laws did not hold true for the behavior of matter and energy in the atomic and sub-atomic level. These laws were not wrong but inadequate. They gave rise in the early twentieth century to a different field of physics, quantum mechanics.

Quantum mechanics reveals that certain phenomenon of the physical world can be described as mysterious or spiritual. This has required science to step across a threshold and embrace another model of reality. It is very different and in some cases contradictory. We are being faced with changes that require us to move away from Newtonian physics, based in materialism and empirical evidence. Human responsibility must include a quantum understanding of the universe. Quantum is spiritual!

We have lived in Newtonian spirituality grounded in the mechanics of doctrine, tradition, institutionalism, and biblical formulae. These are not wrong, just inadequate to equip us to embrace a spirituality governed by relationship rather than by rules. Relational governance is organic rather than organizational; mysterious rather than mechanical; and dynamic rather than dogmatic. These next few years will be demanding!

Summary:
I would love to offer you a road map for the

future and a manual on how to cross this threshold without pain or pressure. However, I haven't got the mystery figured out for myself. If I did, it would most likely be inaccurate, incomprehensible, or inadequate!

Lifechangers feels a deep responsibility to assist you in being prepared for changes in the transition that we, ourselves, are unable to control or ignore. Allow me to share with you the personal posture I have found to be most helpful in navigating the shifting tides of this transitional era.

First, I have demanded of myself that I walk in relational safety. This *Plumbline* is the expression of several men and women who have personally arrived at this posture and seek to walk relationally. This is both personally comforting and correcting. Each of you must find relational safety. Relationships can be risky. Seek a community, large or small, that is focused on pleasing the Father; centered in the all-inclusive Kingdom of Christ; and endeavoring to live by the Agape of God as expressed in His eternal value system[31].

Second, I am seeking to embrace the mystery that is unfolding before us. I find that I am inextricably connected to it, even if I may not fully understand it. New Testament believers walked into a mystery that gradually unfolded to them over time. The mystery is not a thing or a concept. *The Mystery is a Person.*

---

31 I unpack the eternal value system in a series of *Plumblines* available through *Lifechangers*.

He is being revealed throughout all creation. We are appealing to the Cosmic Christ.

Third, I am leaving myself open to a personal and/or Church-wide "rummage sale". There are certain eternal, uncreated realities of God's nature as revealed in Christ Jesus and of His redemptive purpose that are immutable. All else, we must be willing for Him to shake and sort at His pleasure. He will make us able to stand, pleasing Him in the uncertain era that is now unfolding.

May we meet steadfast and secure on the other side of this glorious threshold He is setting before us!

LIFECHANGERS®

P.O. Box 3709 ❖ Cookeville, TN 38502
931.520.3730 ❖ lc@lifechangers.org

www.ingramcontent.com/pod-product-compliance
Lightning Source LLC
Chambersburg PA
CBHW071752020426
42331CB00008B/2289